JOURNEY WITH
SAINT MARY

JOURNEY WITH
SAINT MARY

By Yostina Youssef

Illustrated by Mina Anton

LITTLE FLOCK BOOKS

AN IMPRINT OF ACTS PRESS

LITTLE FLOCK BOOKS
AN IMPRINT OF ACTS PRESS

P · R · E · S · S

http://acts.press

ISBN 978-1-940661-40-7

CONTENTS

CHAPTER I

EARLY LIFE

Saint Mary, the mother of our Lord Jesus Christ, is the daughter of Saints Joachim and Anna of Nazareth. Her parents were righteous, God-loving people, although life was not always easy for them. Even when all hope seemed lost, they never stopped believing that God would hear their prayers.

Saint Anna's family was from the tribe of Levi, the tribe of the priesthood. Saint Joachim, was the great great (many greats) grandson of King David, from the tribe of Judah. Saint Joachim was a successful shepherd, who was faithful to God and always gave to the needy.

Saint Joachim was married at the age of twenty to Saint Anna. They lived together with God's commandments always before them. However, even after fifty years of marriage, Saint Joachim and Saint Anna were unable to have a baby. They never gave up

praying that one day they would.

Saint Joachim and Saint Anna made a special promise to God, called a **vow**. They vowed that if they ever did have a baby, they would dedicate that child to God.

In the olden days, a baby was not only a blessing, but necessary for those waiting for the **Messiah**. The Messiah is the awaited Savior of the world who would save us from our sins. It was very important to the community that women have babies because they were waiting for the Messiah to be born.

Since Saint Joachim and Saint Anna were not blessed with a baby, their community turned away from them. Saint Anna was considered unlucky and even cursed. Even though they were very good people and always followed God's commandments, their people turned their backs on them.

Both Saint Joachim and Saint Anna were very sad and prayed deeply to God. They both retreated from their community for a time to focus on their prayers and ask God for mercy. Saint Joachim went to the mountains and Saint Anna went to her gardens.

Saint Joachim was visited by Archangel Gabriel in the mountains. Archangel Gabriel brought good news, that Saint Joachim would be a father to a daughter named Mary. Just like Abraham was blessed with a special son in his old age, so would Mary be very special, not only to Saint Joachim, but to all humanity.

Archangel Gabriel also visited Saint Anna with this good news in her garden. Saint Anna was told that she would have a daughter named Mary and that she would be blessed above all women. She was instructed to be sure that no unclean things came near the child, because she would be special for God.

Everything that Archangel Gabriel said came true
for the righteous Saints Joachim and Anna. They had
a daughter in their very old age and named her Mary.
The entire community shared in their great joy of finally
having a precious child. Of course, they kept their vow
and presented her to the temple when she was three
years old.

Saint Mary lived and grew up in a special school for girls at the temple. At three years old, she was already serving God by helping around the temple. Saint Mary was dedicated in her lessons to learn the Word of God, always studying more than what was required. She also became accomplished in practical skills, like weaving and wool-work. By the age of eight, both of her parents had died and she became an orphan in the care of the temple.

CHAPTER 2

THE BETR⊙THAL

When Saint Mary was around thirteen, it was her time to leave the temple. It was the tradition of that time for all the girls that came of age to be married to faithful men from the congregation. But Saint Mary wished to keep herself dedicated for the Lord. She did not want to marry a man. Instead, she wanted to stay focused only on her prayers and service to God. The priests of the temple wanted to grant Saint Mary her holy wish, but also wanted protection for her, since she was an orphan. They prayed for God's will to be known.

After much prayer, the priests decided to place Saint Mary in the care of an elderly **widower**. A

widower is a man whose wife has passed away. The priests cast lots to see from which tribe the widower would be chosen. God directed the lot to choose a man from the tribe of Judah. Messages went out to twelve widowers of the tribe of Judah to come to the temple with their rods. One of those widowers was Saint Joseph, a poor, eighty year old carpenter from Nazareth.

The staff or rod of each man was
placed on the altar in the temple
overnight. Through the night,
Saint Mary and the priests
prayed for God's guidance
and blessing in directing
Saint Mary's next steps. The following
morning, the widowers returned to
receive their rods again. On Saint
Joseph's rod, three leaves had blossomed!
This was a sign from God that Saint
Joseph was chosen to take care of
Saint Mary.

The blossoming of a rod is also seen
in the Old Testament. In Numbers
17, we read that the children of
Israel were complaining against
Moses and Aaron in the wilderness.
To demonstrate that Aaron was God's
chosen priest, his rod along with one rod
from someone of each tribe was placed
on the altar. The next day, the rods were
returned to their owners, except for
Aaron's rod that had blossomed and

even produced ripe almonds. The similarities between the rod of Aaron and the rod of Joseph is one way that God declared His will concerning Saint Mary's care.

There is another tradition about Joseph's rod. While Joseph's rod was laying on the altar, a dove landed on it. The dove is seen in many stories as the Holy Spirit, such as the Theophany, when Jesus Christ was baptized in the Jordan River (Matthew 3:13-16). This also demonstrates God's blessings upon Saint Joseph as a caretaker for Saint Mary.

The high priest understood the significance of Saint Joseph's rod and he was elected to betroth Saint Mary. A **betrothal** is an agreement with the purpose to be married in the future. The difference between engagements today and the ancient Jewish tradition is the betrothed couple lived in the same house as husband and wife, but were not legally or physically married.

CHAPTER 3

THE VISITATIONS

After the betrothal, Saint Mary left her room in the temple school and went to live in Saint Joseph's house. One day, Archangel Gabriel appeared to her and told her that she will be the mother of the long awaited Messiah, the Savior of the world. At first, Saint Mary was confused, but she responded to God with humility and grace. Saint Mary answered, "Behold the handmaid of the Lord; let it be to me according to your word" (Luke 1:38).

Archangel Gabriel also told her that her cousin

Elizabeth was pregnant with Saint John the Baptist.
Saint Mary went to visit and stay with her cousin right
away. This was about ninety miles of walking. While
it takes about two hours by car on the freeway today,
it probably took her a few days of travel. Even though
it was difficult to travel, and she herself was already
pregnant with our Lord, her love for her cousin and her
readiness to serve her was more important than any
discomfort.

When Saint Elizabeth first saw her young cousin coming to her, she felt Saint John leap inside her womb. She understood that Saint Mary was blessed above any other woman. Saint Elizabeth knew that her young cousin was chosen by God to hold and raise our Lord Jesus as her Son. Saint Mary stayed with her elderly cousin for three months to take care of her. Her humility and love are shown through this act of compassion for her saintly relative.

Here is the beautiful song of praise that Saint Mary said while visiting Saint Elizabeth:

> *"My soul magnifies the Lord, And my*
> *spirit has rejoiced in God my Savior.*
> *For He has regarded the lowly*
> *state of His maidservant;*
> *For behold, henceforth all*
> *generations will call me blessed.*
> *For He who is mighty has done great*
> *things for me, And holy is His name.*
> *And His mercy is on those who fear*
> *Him from generation to generation.*
> *He has shown strength with His arm;*
> *He has scattered the proud in the*

imagination of their hearts.
He has put down the mighty from their
thrones, And exalted the lowly.
He has filled the hungry with good things,
And the rich He has sent away empty.
He has helped His servant Israel,
In remembrance of His mercy,
As He spoke to our fathers, To
Abraham and to his seed forever."
(Luke 1:46-55)

When we look closely at Saint Mary's song of praise, we see many similarities to the prayer of Hannah, the mother of Prophet Samuel, as well as many Psalms and Proverbs. These similarities show us how well she knew the Scripture. The words of prayer in the Bible became her own words of joy and praise for God. This is a worthy goal, as God told Joshua, "This Book of the Law shall not depart from your mouth, but you shall meditate in it day and night, that you may observe to do according to all that is written in it. For then you will make your way prosperous, and then you will have good success" (Joshua 1:8). We pray to learn from Saint Mary by growing in and following the Word of God, just as she did.

After Saint Joseph learned about Saint Mary's pregnancy, he was very worried for her. But Archangel Gabriel appeared again to assure him that Saint Mary is still a pure virgin and that the Child will be the Savior of the world: "But while he thought about these things, behold, an angel of the Lord appeared to him in a dream, saying, 'Joseph, son of David, do not be afraid to take to you Mary your wife, for that which is conceived in her is of the Holy Spirit. And she will bring forth a Son, and you shall call His name Jesus, for He will save His people from their sins'" (Matthew 1:20-21). Saint Joseph legally married Saint Mary to protect her and the Child Jesus Christ, but they never shared a marriage bed. Saint Joseph's purpose was to be their protecter and provider.

CHAPTER 4

THE NATIVITY OF OUR LORD JESUS CHRIST

Nearing the end of her pregnancy, Saints Joseph, Mary, and Salome, Saint Mary's cousin, had to travel. Salome acted as Saint Mary's midwife. Her duties were to help deliver the baby and take care of the medical needs of the new mother. The group traveled from Nazareth to Bethlehem for the king's **census**. The census is when the government counts how many people are in each city. The trip was long and difficult, taking many days on the dusty road. Even with a donkey, the journey could have been ten days long!

When they finally reached Bethlehem for the census, the city was so crowded. There weren't any empty rooms for them to stay in. So the King of kings was born in a manger, surrounded by hay and barn animals, showing us true humility.

CHRIST IS BORN! LET US GLORIFY HIM!

Saint Mary miraculously gave birth to our Lord Jesus Christ while she was still a chaste woman of God, as she was for the rest of her life. Saint Salome witnessed and wondered at this great miracle. Saint Mary's fervent and dedicated purity is why we call her the **Holy Virgin**. We also call her **Theotokos**, which means the "Mother of God" in Greek.

This Divine birth was prophesied hundreds of years before by Prophet Isaiah, "Therefore the Lord Himself will give you a sign: Behold, the virgin shall conceive and bear a Son, and shall call His name Immanuel" (7:14). A **prophecy** is the telling of an important event that will happen in the future.

The night of Christ's birth, an angel came to shepherds outside the city of Bethlehem. The angel told them, "Do not be afraid, for behold, I bring you good tidings of great joy which will be to all people. For there is born to you this day in the city of David a Savior, who is Christ the Lord. And this will be the sign to you: You will find a Babe wrapped in swaddling cloths, lying in a manger" (Luke 2:10-12). With the angel came a host (which means a large number!) of angels singing, "Glory to God in the highest, and on earth peace, goodwill toward men!" (Luke 2:14). When the shepherds heard and saw this amazing sight, they went right away to see Saint Mary and her Son, the King of kings.

Wise men also came from the East to worship our Lord Jesus Christ. They had studied the Scripture, saw the star shining brightly over Bethlehem, and understood that it was time for the Savior of the world to be incarnate. Incarnate is when God became Man on Earth. They traveled a very great distance to bring gifts of gold, frankincense, and myrrh to the Child Savior and worship Him (Matthew 2:1-12).

All the while, Saint Mary marveled at all the wonderful things she had seen and experienced; her miraculous pregnancy, the worship of shepherds, the journey of the wise men for her newborn Son, and the numerous dreams and messages from angels. She heard God's servants, Saints Simeon and Anna the Prophetess both prophesy that her Son was the awaited Savior. Saint Luke tells us that Saint Mary "kept all these things, pondered them in her heart" (2:51).

She portrays a beautiful example of self-control and wisdom. Saint Mary kept all these observations and miracles quiet in her heart, never boasting or bragging about all the wonders she had seen.

CHAPTER 5

THE JOURNEY TO EGYPT

After Jesus Christ was born in Bethlehem, Saint Joseph was warned in a dream by an angel of the Lord to go to Egypt, to be far away from King Herod. This evil king had heard from the wise men that the Child Jesus was the True King. Herod wanted to be the only king, so he ordered that all the boys, two years old and younger, be killed.

Saint Joseph was directed to flee to Egypt for two reasons. Firstly, to save our Lord Jesus Christ from a death before His appointed time. Secondly, to bless the people of Egypt, as it says in Isaiah 19:19, "In that day there will be an altar to the Lord in the midst of the land of Egypt, and a pillar to the Lord at its border."

When Jesus was about two years old, the Holy

Family traveled to Egypt. The companions consisted of our Lord Jesus Christ, Saint Mary, Saint Joseph, and Saint Salome, who continued to assist Saint Mary. They stayed in Egypt, traveling from place to place, not staying in any one place for very long. They traveled around Egypt for three years and eleven months. To this day, people can still travel the route of the Holy Family through Egypt to follow their steps and receive their blessings.

One of the first places that the Holy Family stopped by was a city called Tel Basta, where the temple of the idol goddess Bastet was located. They passed a well from which Jesus drank water. Since then, the water has been known to cure 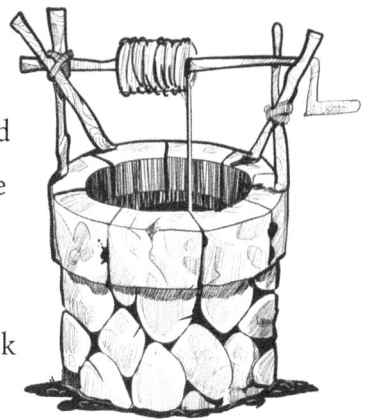 many illnesses. While in Tel Basta, a kind man named Eklom invited the Holy Family to his home for a meal. Our Lord Jesus Christ healed Eklom's wife who had been seriously ill. In her joy from being healed, Eklom's wife wanted to show the Holy Family all of the sights of her city. But when she took them to the temple of the goddess, all the idols fell down and were destroyed in the presence of our Lord Jesus Christ. Because of the anger of the people, the Holy Family left Tel Basta quickly and quietly.

They passed through many cities and towns through Egypt. Another stop was the city of Bilbeis, also called Goshen, where Jacob and his sons lived in Egypt while Joseph was Pharoah's right hand (Genesis 46). There is a tree there to this day that offered shade to the Holy

Family during their stop. Visitors still rest and receive blessings from this ancient tree known as the "Tree of Saint Mary."

The Holy Family then went to Meniet Samannoud, which means "Heel of God". The Lord Jesus rested His foot on a stone and the impression of His foot remained.

The stone was called "Picha Isos" (phonetically) in Coptic, meaning "the heel of Jesus." A monastery was built around it.

From there, they went westward to Wadi El-Natroun or Shiheet, which in Coptic means "scale of hearts." Saint Mary blessed this place and many monasteries are active in this area until this day. Saint Macarius established a monastic community only three hundred years after Saint Mary and our Lord visited this area. Three hundred years may seem like a long time, but when one considers that the Church is two thousand years old, it's actually a short time. Many of our desert fathers and beloved monks came from and lived in this region, including Saint Pishoy, Saint John the Short, Saint Moses the Strong, and Saint Arsenius.

One of their longer stays was in Al-Maady, which might have been up to a month long visit. Here, the

Holy Family sailed from the banks of the Nile River. The place on the river is near to where it is said that Pharaoh's daughter took Moses in his basket. On March 12, 1976, an open book was found floating along the Nile River near the church there. When they retrieved the book, they found that it was a Bible open to the verse of Isaiah 19:25, "Blessed is Egypt My people." This was considered a blessing from God for the Coptic Orthodox Church and the Bible has been preserved in glass and is still visited to this day.

One of the last places the Holy Family took refuge in was Al-Ashmoneen where they stayed for several days. Afterwards they went to Mount Qosqam where a monastery for Saint Mary was later built, also known as El-Moharrak monastery. This monastery is said to be geographically in the center of Egypt, fulfilling the prophecy of Isaiah, "There will be an altar to the Lord in the midst of the land of Egypt" (19:19).

Finally after almost four years, the angel told Joseph that it was safe to go back home, just as the prophecy in Hosea 11:1 says, "Out of Egypt I have called my Son." Saint Mary raised Jesus in Nazareth where he practiced carpentry with Joseph. "And the Child grew and became strong in spirit, filled with wisdom; and the grace of God was upon Him" (Luke 2:40).

CHAPTER 6

DURING JESUS' MINISTRY

Not much is written in the Bible about Jesus' childhood in Nazareth, but there is one amazing story from when He was twelve years old in Luke 2:41-52. Jesus had stayed behind in the temple when the rest of his extended family traveled back to Nazareth. After three days of searching and asking everyone if they'd seen Him, Saint Mary and Saint Joseph finally found him in the temple discussing deep issues with the teachers.

"So when they saw Him, they were amazed; and His mother said to Him, 'Son, why have You done this to us? Look, Your father and I have sought You anxiously'" (Luke 2:48). She had been very worried about her Son while at the same time so proud and amazed at what he was preaching and teaching to the teachers.

Then He went down with them and went back to
Nazareth. He listened and obeyed His parents until it
was time for Him to leave home and begin His ministry.
It is important to understand that our Lord Jesus
Christ, Who commanded us to honor our parents, was
obedient to His own mother. Even though He is her
Creator, He obeyed Saint Mary as any child does with
his mother, with complete humility.

"His mother kept all these things in her heart. And
Jesus increased in wisdom and stature, and in favor
with God and men" (Luke 2:51-52). She raised the King
of kings as her own Son, even though she was poor.

God found her worthy and she loved her Lord, always a model of virtues and goodness. Again, we find that she never bragged or boasted about all the amazing wonders of her Son and Lord. Instead, she stayed quiet and humble, waiting and watching to see what God had in store for humanity.

In the journey through Egypt, our Lord performed many miracles that have been told to us through tradition. But the first miracle of our Lord's ministry that is mentioned in the Bible was at the wedding in Cana of Galilee. This miracle happened because of the intercession of Saint Mary. Intercession is when the saints pray to God for us.

Saint Mary noticed that the hosts of the wedding had run out of wine. She told our Lord Jesus Christ, "They have no wine." Our Lord told her, "My hour has not yet come," meaning He wasn't ready to perform public signs yet. But because of her request, He performed this amazing miracle. His mother knew He would not say no to her, so she told the servants, "Whatever He tells you, do it." He told them to fill six large pots with water, and when they poured them out, they found the water was transformed into wine (John 2:1-12).

This miracle is so significant that we celebrate it on Tubah 13 or January 21 every year as a minor feast of the Lord. It also shows us the effect of Saint Mary's intercessions for us. Although Jesus was reluctant to show His power at the wedding, He did so because His mother asked on behalf of the hosts of the wedding. Always remember that Saint Mary is our mother too. When we ask for her help, we can count on her prayers to strengthen our own prayers.

Through the Gospel, we often see Saint Mary following our Lord's ministry and being near Him, even to the Cross. In the Ninth Hour of the Agpeya, we pray, "When the mother saw the Lamb and Shepherd, the Savior of the world, hung on the Cross, she said while weeping, 'The world rejoices in receiving salvation, while my heart burns as I look at Your crucifixion which You are enduring for the sake of all, my Son and my God.'" Can you imagine her sadness and heartbreak at seeing her Son hurt and murdered on the Cross?

Our Savior loved His mother so much that, even through the pain He suffered on the Cross, He made sure she would be cared for. He told Saint John, the disciple He loved, to take care of His mother and treat

her as his own mother. Likewise, Saint Mary was to
treat Saint John as her own son. She stayed with Saint
John and the disciples until her death according to
John 19:25-27. By giving her as a mother to one of His
disciples, our Lord Jesus Christ gives Saint Mary as a
mother to all of us.

As Saint Mary was present for her Son's death, she also witnessed His Resurrection on Sunday morning. In Luke 24:1-2 we read, "Now  on the first day of the week, very early in the morning, they, and certain other women with them, came to the tomb bringing the spices which they had prepared. But they found the stone rolled away from the tomb." Inside the tomb they found the angels who told them the good news, "He is not here, but is risen!" (Luke 24:6) Imagine Saint Mary's great joy, after having suffered so deeply from watching her Son die on the cross, to hear and see this wonderful fulfillment of God's promise of salvation!

CHAPTER 7

LIFE IN THE EARLY CHURCH

S aint Mary lived with Saint John for fourteen years, ministering to the young Church and being a mother to all. She was at the gathering in the Upper Room with the disciples when they chose Matthias to replace Judas Iscariot as the twelfth disciple (Acts 1:12-14).

Saint Mary was also there on the Feast of Pentecost in Acts 2 when the Holy Spirit filled the apostles, appearing as tongues of fire on each of them. Icons of the Pentecost always have Saint Mary in the center of the group, representing her important role in the Early Church.

One time Saint Mary traveled to a prison, where Saint Matthias had been arrested. The governor had put him in jail after many people in the town converted to Christianity. In their zeal for their new faith, the new Christians had destroyed many of the idols of the town, which made the governor very angry. Saint Mary came and prayed for Saint Matthias outside of his cell and the iron bars melted! Not only did the iron in the jail melt away, but all the iron throughout the city. When the governor witnessed the power behind Saint Mary's intercession, he asked for her help because his son was ill. Of course Saint Mary prayed for the young boy and he was blessed with perfect health. The governor destroyed the rest of the idols himself and built a church in honor of Saint Mary.

About ten years after the ascension of our Lord Jesus Christ, Herod began the persecution of Christians. Saint John the Beloved took Saint Mary to Ephesus to keep her safe. From there she continued to write letters of encouragement and comfort. She also visited the believers, sometimes traveling great distances by sea and land.

Believers, both newly baptized and those who had been with Christ our Lord from the beginning, all wished to be near and hear the voice of Saint Mary. They traveled from all over to visit her and receive comfort from her. She did not show partiality or favoritism, but  showed love to every person who wished to see her. She healed the sick, strengthened the weak, and comforted the sorrowful. Most importantly, she confirmed the faith of the believers, giving them joy and love and strengthening their hope. Saint Mary was a mother, teacher, and role model in the Early Church, exactly as she is for us today.

CHAPTER 8

THE DORMITION AND THE APPARITIONS

When Saint Mary was around sixty years old, she once again received a message from God. He told her that in three days she would join her Son in Heaven. The apostles gathered together to say goodbye. They witnessed a bright light as our Lord Jesus Christ and a host of angels received Saint Mary's soul at her death. The passing away or falling asleep of Saint Mary is called her **dormition**. Her body was buried at the Mount of Olives in the Garden of Gethsemane with her parents and Saint Joseph.

The Jews understood Saint Mary's significance to the congregation of the Early Church. They wished to take her body away in order to hurt the Christian movement. Some of the Jews tried to prevent the apostles from burying her body, but without success.

According to the Coptic Orthodox Synaxarium,
"One of the Jews seized the coffin with his hands,
which were separated instantly from his body and they
remained attached to the coffin. He regretted his evil
deed and wept bitterly. Through the supplications of the
saintly apostles, his hands were reattached to his body,
and he believed in the Lord Christ." Tradition tells us

that this man was the sick man that Jesus healed by the pool of Bethesda. Jesus had told him, "See, you have been made well. Sin no more, lest a worse thing come upon you" (John 5:14).

Saint Thomas had been preaching in India at the time of Saint Mary's dormition. He was not in Jerusalem when she departed to Heaven. However, he saw the body of Saint Mary being carried away by angels. When Saint Thomas returned to Jerusalem several months later, he asked the other disciples if he could see where they buried her. They opened the tomb for Saint Thomas' benefit, but found the tomb empty. Saint Thomas then explained to the disciples what he had seen while in India. The event of Saint Mary's body being carried to Heaven after her death is called the **assumption** or **translation**.

The disciples wanted to see the same miracle that Saint Thomas witnessed. So they all fasted for two weeks together until they also saw the Holy Virgin's body being carried up by angels! The Coptic Orthodox Church continues the tradition of fasting for two weeks every August to remember this miracle.

It is important to remember that the congregation of saints in Heaven still belong to the Church along with the congregation of the believers on Earth. We are all One Body of Christ together, the saints in Heaven and the believers still striving for Heaven today. Saint Mary's intercessions and presence in our Church is witnessed throughout the history of the Church.

On April 2, 1968, our Holy Mother, Saint Mary,
appeared at Saint Mary's Church in Zeitoun, Egypt.
Zeitoun is a suburb in the city of Cairo, the capital of
Egypt. Historically, this church is on the route that
the Holy Family traveled during their stay in Egypt.
The holy appearance of a saint after death is called an
apparition.

The apparition of Saint Mary continued for many months, sometimes every day, and for many hours at a time. Saint Mary appeared sometimes kneeling at the cross, sometimes holding Child Jesus Christ. Oftentimes, doves flew around her.

This miracle was witnessed by thousands of people, of every religion, nationality, and rank. She blessed the people with the movement of her hand and her head. His Holiness St. Pope Kyrillos the Sixth affirmed this great miracle. The fruit of the apparitions was that many people were renewed in their faith, repented, and confessed. Another fruit of this great miracle was that it led to many amazing healings that astonished doctors and scientists.

There are many other apparitions of Saint Mary all over the world, in churches and villages. She usually appears to provide spiritual encouragement or physical healing to those who call on her.

CHAPTER 9

TITLES AND SYMBOLS

Saint Mary is our most beloved and fervent intercessor. She is included in many of our Orthodox prayers and hymns. She has many titles and descriptions in the Church, including:

"**Theotokos**," which means "Mother of God" in Greek. It is the most common name for Saint Mary. The Early Church Fathers tell us how important it is to call her "Mother of God." This is because by calling her the "Mother of God," we are saying that we believe that God was incarnate and born as perfect God and perfect man in the Nativity.

We also call Saint Mary the "**Second Heaven**" because Heaven is the home of God. When Christ was in her womb, she became His heaven on Earth. Saint Mary carried our Lord, Who also dwells in Heaven. Also, in Coptic icons, she is often is wearing blue with stars to remind us of this title.

Saint Mary is also called the **"Golden Lampstand"** because, just like a lampstand holds candles, Saint Mary carried Christ, the Light of the World Who enlightens the whole world! The lampstand is gold to show its purity and greatness, exactly as Saint Mary is pure and great.

Especially during the blessed Coptic month of Kiahk, we call Saint Mary the **"Burning Bush."** Kiahk is the Coptic month during which we fast to prepare for, and celebrate, the birth of Christ our Savior. We praise our Lord Jesus Christ for coming to Earth and taking flesh from the Holy Virgin Mary. There is a special hymn that explains this title, which can be found in the next chapter.

We call Saint Mary "**Aaron's rod**" that budded without planting or watering (Deuteronomy 10:3-5; Hebrews 9:4). The miraculous rod brought forth fruit (Numbers 17:6-8), when it seemed to be dead or cut off. This is a symbol for the Virgin Mary who gave birth to the Child Jesus miraculously by the Holy Spirit.

"**Jacob's Ladder**" is another title for Saint Mary. In the Old Testament, Jacob fell asleep on a rock and dreamt of a ladder that reached to Heaven, with angels going up and down the ladder singing praises to God. Saint Mary is Jacob's ladder, because by giving birth to Christ, she allows us to reach heaven and sing praises to God forever with the angels (Genesis 28:10-12).

Saint Mary is also called the "**Golden Censer**" or "**Aaron's Censer.**" Just like a censer carries incense that spreads a nice aroma or fragrance, Saint Mary carried our Lord Christ whose love spreads to all people, to save us from our sins. Just as with the Golden Lampstand, the censer is gold that symbolizes purity and greatness, which is again represented in Saint Mary.

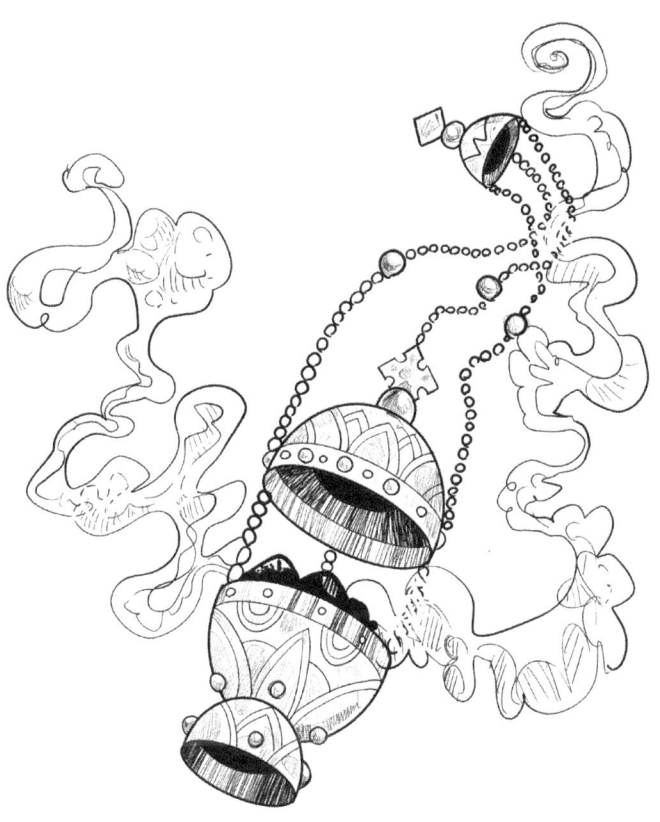

We also call Saint Mary the **"Tabernacle of Moses"** or **"True Tabernacle"** in reference to the meeting place of God in the Old Testament. This title fits Saint Mary, because her body held God and allows all of us to meet Him as well. The tabernacle was built to God's specifications and of the best material. In the same way, Saint Mary is so full of virtue and is the best of humanity.

CHAPTER 10

HYMNS AND PRAISES

There are many other titles we use in our praises for Saint Mary, especially during the **Midnight Psalmody (Tasbeha)**. During the Midnight Psalmody (Tasbeha), the congregation prays late at night or very early in the morning in preparation for the Divine Liturgy. The structure of the hymns are arranged in four canticles, or songs of praise, in addition to doxologies and songs from the Bible.

A **doxology** is a song of praise, taken from the Greek word for glorification.

A doxology for Saint Mary has a special name, the **Theotokion** (single) or **Theotokia** (plural). There is a different Theotokion for every day of the week and each one contains many titles and attributes of Saint Mary.

Sunday

The Sunday Theotokion is definitely the longest with seventeen sections, the eighth one being the familiar "Shere ne Maria" or "Hail to You, Mary," that lists many of her titles. Some of those titles are "the unfading crown," "the daughter of King David," and "the joy of all generations."

Monday

In the Monday Theotokion, the Church describes how Saint Mary became the "new Eve." Eve, the first woman ever created, was the mother of all humanity. However, Saint Mary is the new mother of humanity by delivering Christ, Who is our salvation and redemption. The repeating refrain is "He shone in the flesh, taken from the Virgin, without the seed of man, in order to save us."

Tuesday

In the Tuesday Theotokion, the focus shifts to the Divine conception of our Lord Jesus Christ in the womb of Saint Mary. The refrain is "For of His own will, and the pleasure of His Father, and the Holy Spirit, He came and saved us." Saint Mary became pregnant through the Grace of God for the salvation of all of us. God was pleased to give this sacrifice of His Son for us because of His love for us.

Wednesday

In the Wednesday Theotokion, the Church honors Saint Mary and blesses her above all others. The refrain says, "The Father looked from heaven, and found no one like you, He sent His Only Begotten, who came and took flesh from you." An important point to remember, is that God sees all time — past, present, and future — at once. When "the Father looked from Heaven" and found no one like Saint Mary, it is saying that Saint Mary is the best of all humanity in all time.

Thursday

In the Thursday Theotokion, the Church explains the Incarnation of Jesus Christ. Even though Jesus

Christ was born as a Man, He was God before, during, and after the birth of Saint Mary, His Divinity never changed. "He did not cease [stop] to be divine, He came and became the Son of Man, for He is the true God, who came and saved us."

Friday

In the Friday Theotokion, the Church honors Saint Mary's role in bringing Christ to us to heal our separation from God. The refrain explains, "He took what is ours, and gave us what is His. We praise and glorify Him, and exalt Him." Our Savior Jesus Christ took our sin and gave us the Holy Spirit. A very uneven trade made from His love for us!

Saturday

In the Saturday Theotokion, the Church praises Saint Mary for giving birth to Christ and repeats some of the greeting of Archangel Gabriel to her in the Annunciation. The refrain is "Hail to you O full of grace, Hail to you who has found grace, Hail to you who has given birth to Christ, the Lord is with you." May we always join the angels in praising our beloved mother and never stop asking for her intercessions.

Each of the seven Theotokia is a praise and honor for Saint Mary. In each doxology, the Church offers us a glimpse of the magnificence of her virtues and love for our Lord Jesus Christ and for each of us. By singing and praying these hymns for her, we become closer to her and seek her intercessions with her Son for us.

DAILY PRAYERS

We also honor Saint Mary in our daily prayers, one example is in the introduction to the Creed in the Agpeya. We begin with "We exalt you, the Mother of the true Light, and we glorify you, O saint and Theotokos, for you brought forth unto us the Savior of the whole world." Also we pray for her intercessions throughout the Divine Liturgy.

OTHER PRAISES

Outside of the liturgical tradition, there are many songs of praise for Saint Mary. In fact, it seems every year a new song of praise is being written for our beloved mother. Below is a small collection of praises that venerate Saint Mary the Theotokos.

The first selection is called the Burning Bush and is sung during the month of Kiahk while we fast in preparation for the Feast of the Nativity. The Midnight Psalmody during this blessed month is expanded with each of the seven Theotokia. That's why the Arabic name for the collection of praises in English translates to **"Seven and Four,"** signifying the seven Theotokia and the four canticles, or songs of praise. This hymn

explains how the Burning Bush that Moses saw in the
Old Testament is an illustration of our beloved mother,
Saint Mary:

> *The Burning Bush seen by Moses*
> *The prophet in the wilderness*
> *The fire inside, it was aflame*
> *But never consumed or injured it*

The same with the Theotokos Mary
Carried the fire of divinity
Nine months in her holy body
Without blemishing her virginity

The second is the annual praise for Saint Mary, which refers to the censer that is used in the church. The censer spreads the sweet-smelling aroma of incense during the Divine Liturgy. This praise reminds us of Saint Mary's title of the Golden Censer. It is chanted in the Divine Liturgy before the reading of the Pauline Epistle. It is followed by a verse of intercession for Saint Mary:

This censer of pure gold,
Bearing the aroma,
Is in the hands of Aaron the priest,
Offering up incense upon the altar

Through the intercessions,
of the Mother of God Saint Mary,
O Lord grant us,
the forgiveness of our sins.

The last song shared is one that might be sung in Sunday School or a prayer meeting. It is not sung during Tasbeha or Liturgy, but is often sung in the hearts of those who trust Saint Mary as their faithful intercessor.

Hail to Mary, mother of God
From sunrise, to sunset
Magnify her, glorify her
Put her always in your heart

She has born onto us
The Savior of the world
He came and saved our souls
And forgave us our sins

She is the Lady, and the virgin
Our Queen in heaven
She's above the Cherubim
And praised by the Seraphim

She is famous and well-known
As the best shelter to rest
Try her and you will find that
For your help, she's always there

Please, O Mary, pray for us
And sinners to return
Teach us and guide all of us
For you are the faithful saint

CHAPTER II

FEASTS OF SAINT MARY

In the Coptic Orthodox Church we always celebrate the day that a saint passes away because that is when they receive their eternal reward to be with our Lord Jesus Christ forever in Heaven. We celebrate Saint Mary's passing on the 21st of Toba (January 29). This day is so important that we commemorate Saint Mary's passing on the 21st day of every Coptic month!

We also celebrate the day when the apostles witnessed the translation of Saint Mary's body on the 16th of the Coptic month of Mesra (August 22nd). We remember this day after fasting for

two weeks, keeping withinin the tradition of the great miracle seen by the disciples.

We also have many other feasts and remembrances for the Holy Virgin Mary throughout the Coptic calendar. For example, the entire month of Kiahk is full of praises for Saint Mary in preparation for the Feast of the Nativity. The month of Kiahk typically has four weekends, in which the "Seven and Four" are sung the night before the Liturgy. If the parish church is able, the service finishes with a Liturgy in the very early hours of the morning. We honor Saint Mary for delivering the Savior of the world to us and pray for her intercessions to her Son.

Listed below are her feasts in chronological order of her life:

* Mesra 7 (August 13) - Annunciation of the birth of the Blessed Virgin Mary to her parents Saint Joachim and Saint Anna

* Bashons 1 (May 9) - The nativity, or birth, of the Theotokos, Saint Mary

* Kiahk 3 (December 12) - The entry of the most Holy Theotokos into the temple at Jerusalem as a child

* Bashons 24 (June 1) - The arrival of the Holy Family in Egypt

* Toba 21 (January 29) - The dormition of our Lady, the Theotokos; this celebration is repeated on the 21st of every Coptic month

* Mesra 16 (August 22) - The translation of Saint Mary's body to Heaven, which ends the two week Fast for Saint Mary

* Paona 21 (June 28) - Dedication of the first Church for the All-Holy and blessed Virgin Mary in the city of Ephesus, where she lived with Saint John the Beloved

* Baramhat 24 (April 2) - The apparition of the Theotokos in Zeitoun in 1968

WORKS CITED

A Guide to Kiahk Praises. 2nd Ed., Edited by Fr. Markos Hanna. Saint Mark Coptic Orthodox Church, Los Angeles. Mina Printing, 1999.

Abdelsayed, Fr. John Paul; Malaty, Fr. Tadros Yacoub. *Sayings of the Fathers on the Holy Theotokos*. Saint Paul Brotherhood Press, 2015.

Bishop Demetrius. *The Visit of the Holy Family*. 2nd Ed., Translated by Adeeb Makar. Coptic Orthodox Diocese of Mallawi.

"Coptic Synaxarium". *Coptic Orthodox Heritage*. Saint Takla Haymanout Website: General Portal for the Coptic Orthodox Church Faith, Egypt, https://st-takla.org

"Coptic Synaxarium". *Coptic Orthodox Church Network*, Saint Mark Coptic Church, New Jersey, 2014, https://CopticChurch.net

H.H. Pope Shenouda. *The Holy Virgin Saint Mary.* Orthodox Coptic Clerical College, Cairo. Anba Rueiss Press, 1999.

The Coptic Book of Hours. Edited by Fr. Matthias Wahba. Saint Antonius Coptic Church, Hayward. Al Geil Printing House, 1994.

The Holy Bible. New King James Version. Thomas Nelson Publishers, 1975. BibleGateway.com, Web. April 2019.

The Holy Psalmody. Ridgewood, New York. Saint Mary and Saint Antonios Coptic Orthodox Church.

The Life of the Virgin Mary, the Theotokos. Buena Vista, Colorado. Holy Apostles' Convent, 1989.

Made in the USA
Middletown, DE
19 August 2020